Timeline of ancient Greece

3200–1100 BC

In the Bronze Age, metal is used for the first time, and the first civilisations appear. On islands in the Aegean Sea, Greeks build towns and huge palaces. The first Greek-speaking people settle in mainland Greece. An early system of writing is used, and the written history of Greece begins.

40,000 BC

The first people settle in Greece, hunting and gathering food. These early communities live in temporary campsites, often inside caves and rock shelters.

1100–800 BC

Greece enters a time of unrest and hardship known as the Dark Ages.

6500–3200 BC

The nomadic lifestyle of the hunter-gatherers gradually disappears as people settle down in one place. A new period of human history begins, called the Neolithic (New Stone Age). The first villages are built and the first pottery is made.

c. 775 BC

The Greek alphabet is invented.

800–500 BC

Greece enters a period of recovery, known as the Archaic period. Greek society begins to develop: population increases, cities such as Athens, Olympia and Sparta become major centres.

500–323 BC

This Classical period, or 'golden age', is marked by the blossoming of Greek culture. The best Greek poets, playwrights, historians, philosophers, doctors, public speakers, astronomers, mathematicians, scientists and statesmen live and work during this time. It ends with the death of Alexander the Great in 323 BC.

146 BC

Mainland Greece becomes a province of the Roman Empire. The dominance of the ancient Greek civilisation comes to an end.

776 BC

The first Olympic Games are held.

c. 590 BC

The first Greek coins are minted.

Map of ancient Greece

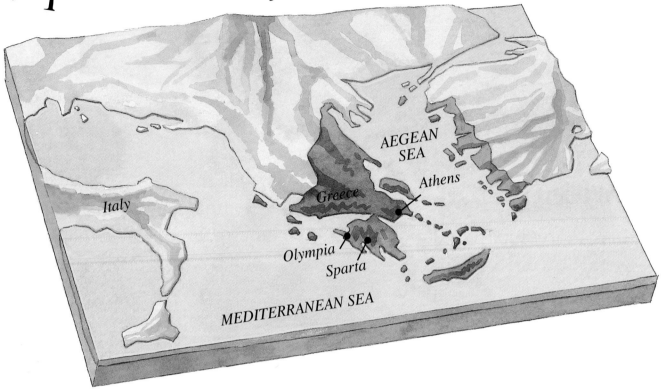

In ancient times very few people lived in inland Greece, because it was mountainous and not very good for farming. Most Greeks lived near the sea, as many still do today. Along much of the coast there was a narrow plain that could be cultivated. Because the mountains made land travel difficult, the Greeks became a people of the sea. Sailing was needed for contact with neighbours, for fishing and for long-distance trading. The Greeks triumphed over the challenges of their landscape. For example, there were few large trees, so timber was in short supply. As a result, Greeks made fine temples and statues of stone. They also learned to produce grapes in the shallow soil of hillsides.

Author:
Fiona Macdonald studied history at
Cambridge University and at the University of
East Anglia. She has taught in adult education,
schools and colleges, and is the author of
numerous books for children on historical topics.

Artist:
David Antram was born in Brighton in 1958.
He studied at Eastbourne College of Art and then
worked in advertising for 15 years before
becoming a full-time artist. He has illustrated
many children's non-fiction books.

Series Creator:
David Salariya was born in Dundee,
Scotland. He has illustrated a wide range of books
and has created and designed many new series for
publishers both in the UK and overseas. In 1989
he established The Salariya Book Company. He
lives in Brighton with his wife, the illustrator
Shirley Willis, and their son, Jonathan.

Editor:
Karen Barker Smith

Editorial Assistant:
Stephanie Cole

Published in Great Britain in MMXIV by
Book House, an imprint of
The Salariya Book Company Ltd
25 Marlborough Place, Brighton BN1 1UB
www.salariya.com
www.book-house.co.uk

PB ISBN-13: 978-1-909645-26-4

S A L A R I Y A

A CIP catalogue record for this book is available
from the British Library.

Printed and bound in Singapore.

Visit our website at www.book-house.co.uk
or go to www.salariya.com for **free** electronic versions of:
You Wouldn't Want to be an Egyptian Mummy!
You Wouldn't Want to be a Roman Gladiator!
You Wouldn't Want to be a Polar Explorer!
You Wouldn't Want to sail on a 19th-Century Whaling Ship!

PAPER FROM
SUSTAINABLE
FORESTS

You Wouldn't Want to Be a Slave in Ancient Greece!

Written by
Fiona Macdonald

Illustrated by
David Antram

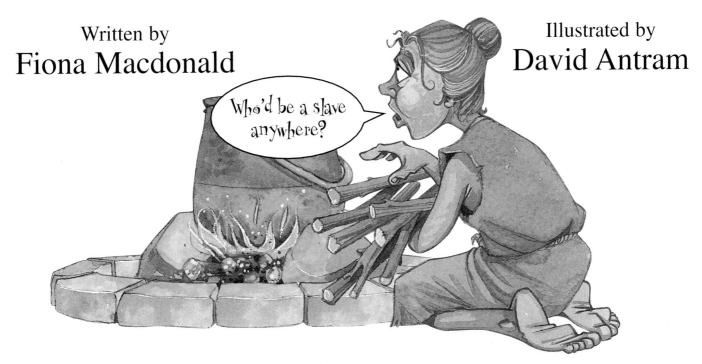

Who'd be a slave anywhere?

A Life You'd Rather Not Have

Created and designed by
David Salariya

BOOK HOUSE
a SALARIYA imprint

Contents

Introduction

It is the 5th century BC and you live just north of the Black Sea, in a Scythian tribe. Your men are famous for their fighting skills and your women lead independent lives. Like many rich Scythian people you are a nomad, travelling from place to place. Occasionally, you visit one of the trading ports on the Black Sea coast. There you meet people from many different lands, including sailors from Greek cities around the Mediterranean Sea. They look at you in astonishment. They are not used to seeing women wearing trousers or walking freely down the streets. They call you a savage.

The ancient Greeks think that all other peoples are less civilised than themselves. They do not understand foreign customs and traditions. Greek artists and architects have created wonderful buildings, statues and pottery and Greek doctors, scientists and thinkers have made many important discoveries. However, these achievements hide a shocking secret: ancient Greek society depends on slavery! Without slaves, the Greeks would have no time for art and scholarship. Slaves already make up a quarter of the population in many Greek cities. Although they are surrounded by a brilliant civilisation, slaves' lives are often grim. You really wouldn't want to be a slave in ancient Greece!

Captured! Seized by slave traders

What you'll leave behind:

WIDE OPEN SPACES. Say goodbye to the vast plains and forests of your homeland.

POSSESSIONS. You will have your weapons and your jewellery taken away.

HOME SWEET HOME. This is the last time you'll see your cosy felt tents or wooden huts.

In the trading port, you hear an alarming rumour – Greek slave traders are near by! The traders trap people and sell them as slaves. They also buy prisoners from warlords who have captured enemies in battle and children from poor families who cannot afford to feed them. You decide to hurry home, but it's too late – you are ambushed and your whole family is captured! Hands bound, you are marched on board a slave-ship.

Get a move on!

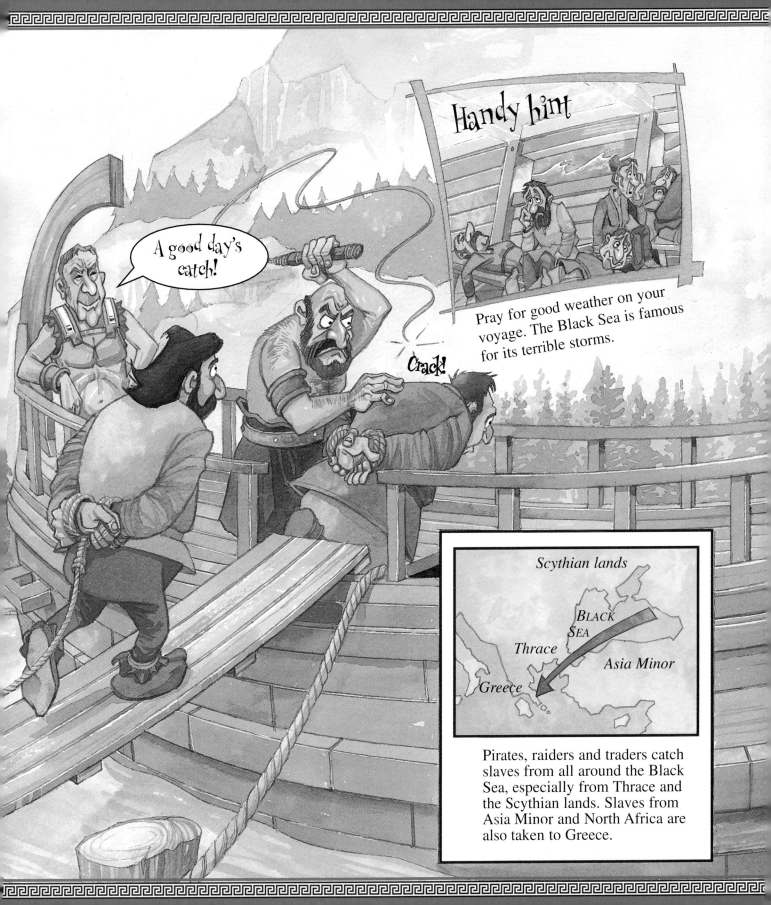

Up for grabs!
On sale in the slave market

You have arrived in Athens, the largest and most powerful city in Greece. About 350,000 people live here and in the surrounding countryside; over 100,000 of them are slaves. The trader takes you to the slave-market in the *agora* (market place). There, you are put on display alongside other men, women and children. Business is brisk – thousands of slaves can be sold here in a single morning. However, prices are low compared to Greek citizens' wages. A skilled workman can earn at least 1 drachma per day. The cheapest slaves are sold for 70 drachmas and the most expensive fetch 300 drachmas – good value for a lifetime's work!

Who else is on sale?

ABANDONED BABY GIRLS are looked after by slave-dealers until they are old enough to sell.

DEBTORS are sold as slaves by the people they owe money to.

DEFEATED ENEMIES are brought here straight from the battlefield. Some are still badly injured.

Parted forever!

Where your family goes:

Before   After

YOUR HUSBAND used to train horses. Now he mends the roads.

YOUR SON used to play outdoors. Now he works inside in a potter's workshop.

YOUR DAUGHTER was a quiet, shy girl. Now she's forced to dance and sing to entertain men at drinking parties.

YOU were a respected member of your tribe. Now you're just a miserable household slave.

Becoming a slave means saying goodbye to your family. You will probably never see them again. Your new owner will only be interested in the work you do. Try to forget that you ever had a husband and children – it's tough, but you'll find it easier to cope with your new life that way. You'll feel lonely, but that's normal for a slave, especially a *xenos* (foreigner).

Your new owner may give orders for your hair to be cut off – short hair is a sign of slavery. He may also mark your arms and neck with tattoos, or even brand you with a hot iron.

Most slaves are surrounded by people who do not speak their language or share their beliefs. They are not allowed to marry. If a female slave has a love-affair and has a baby, she could be forced to abandon it on a rubbish-heap, especially if it's a girl.

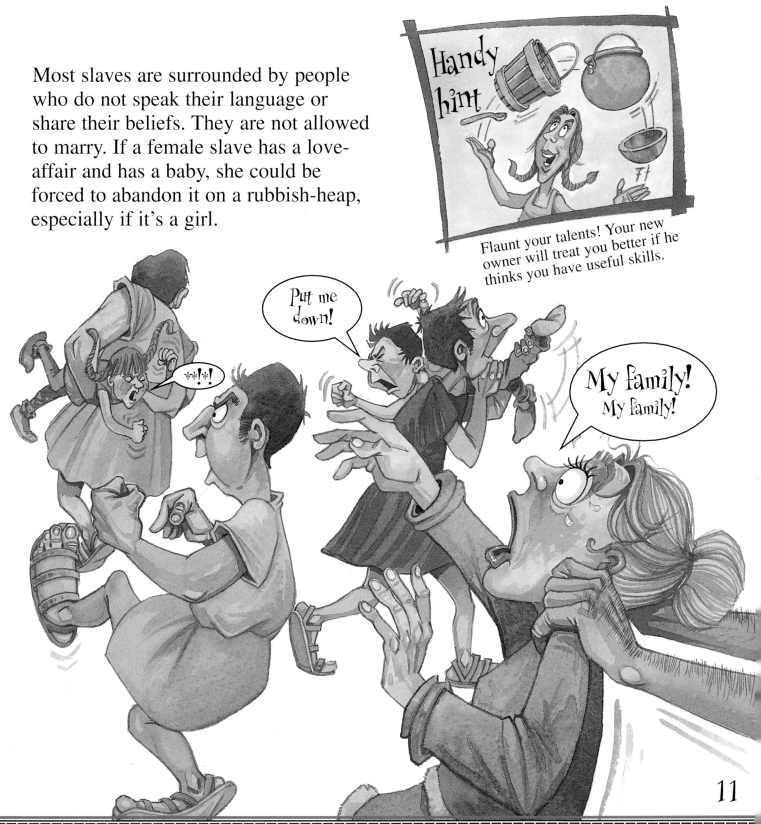

Handy hint

Flaunt your talents! Your new owner will treat you better if he thinks you have useful skills.

11

Back breaking! Household chores

Daily tasks:

SCRUBBING AND SWEEPING takes hours each day. Your knees will ache and creak as you crawl across the cold, tiled floor.

Captured women are always needed in ancient Greece, to work as *oiketai* (household slaves). You do all the daily tasks, such as cooking, cleaning, lighting fires and collecting firewood. You have brushes, mops and rags to help you, and cold water, sand and salt to use for cleaning.

STICKY FINGERS. You have to make fresh bread for each evening meal. Don't add too much water – you might never get free from the dough!

KEEP STIRRING! Your owner's family likes porridge for breakfast. Try not to burn it or make it lumpy or they won't feed you at all!

Who'd be a slave?

Ho hum...

12

Back in your own home, you were used to organising your own time and deciding which tasks to do. But here, you'll be at the beck and call of your owner's wife. She'll give you orders and scold you if she's not happy with your work.

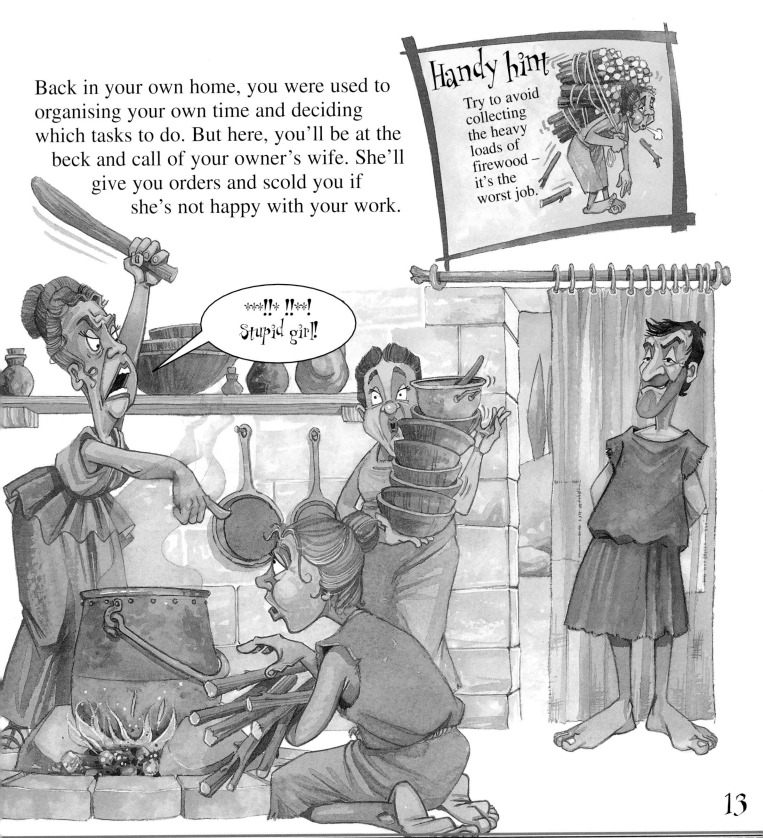

Handy hint
Try to avoid collecting the heavy loads of firewood – it's the worst job.

***!!* !!**! Stupid girl!

Personal services

The ancient Greeks like clean, healthy bodies and admire beauty. But they can't achieve either by themselves. They need slaves to help them bathe, dress and arrange their hair. As part of your work as a female slave, you may also be asked to massage your owner or his wife with olive oil. It's certainly good for soothing their aches and pains, but it's a very messy task. Female slaves are also expected to provide care 24 hours a day for their owner's children. You have to wash them, feed them and get up in the night when they cry. You feel exhausted, but no-one cares because you're just a slave.

AARRGHH!

Beauty duties:

IT TAKES HOURS to arrange an elaborate hairstyle for your owner's wife and you have to stand the whole time.

You look gorgeous!

DON'T TELL your owner's teenage daughter that she's ugly or vain. It's your job to praise her, however she looks!

BATHTIME IS BLISS for your owner's wife, but hard work for her slaves, who have to carry the huge jars of water.

Handy hint

Kept awake at night by a screaming baby? Consult a wise woman for a herbal potion to help the baby sleep.

WHICH IS WORSE – your owner's dirty, dusty feet, or your aching back as you bend down to tie his sandals on?

THE LATEST FASHION – scent made with civet, from wild cats! You hate the smell, but have to sprinkle it on your owner's wife.

PALE AND INTERESTING – that's the style for rich women. As a slave, you'll get sunburnt carrying the sunshade.

No time to spare!

You will find that slave women have no spare time. When you're not busy with cooking, housework or child-care, you are expected to spin woollen thread, weave it into cloth, and sometimes embroider it as well. Each household makes all the cloth it needs for clothes, rugs, cushions, blankets and wall hangings.

In a spin? Working with wool

BOWED DOWN. You may be sent to unload the heavy fleeces which arrive at your owner's house by donkey.

BUZZ BUZZ! You'll find that sheep's wool is tangled up with twigs, dung and live insects, which all need to be washed out.

GREEK CLOTHES are made to fit. Check sizes carefully before you start weaving to ensure the finished cloth is the right size.

IF YOU TANGLE the threads or embroider the wrong pattern you'll have to stay up all night, unpicking your work.

My hair!

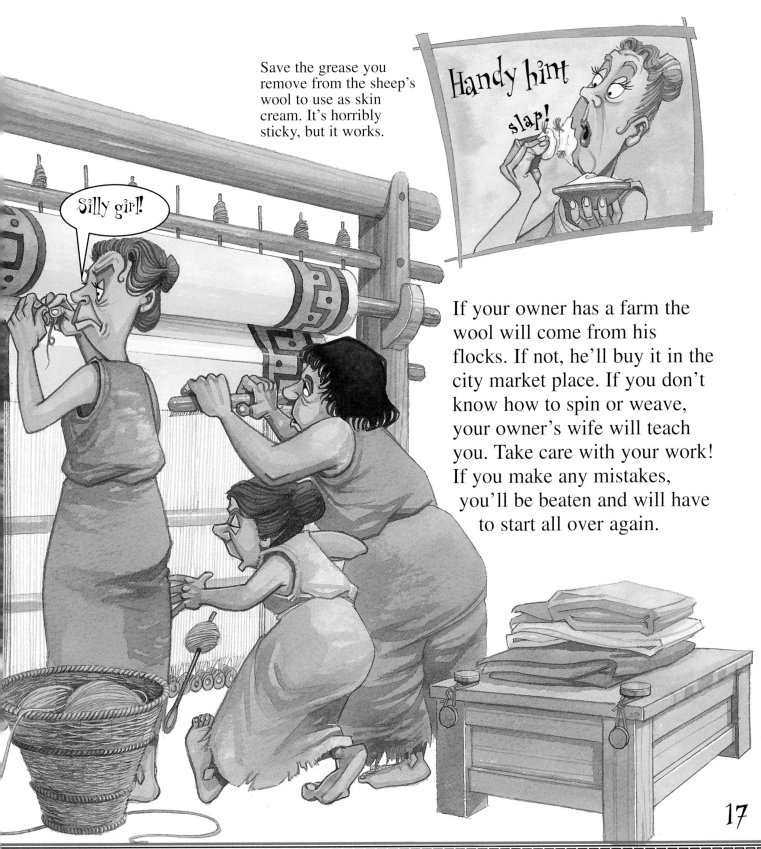

Save the grease you remove from the sheep's wool to use as skin cream. It's horribly sticky, but it works.

Handy hint slap!

Silly girl!

If your owner has a farm the wool will come from his flocks. If not, he'll buy it in the city market place. If you don't know how to spin or weave, your owner's wife will teach you. Take care with your work! If you make any mistakes, you'll be beaten and will have to start all over again.

17

Fetching and carrying – city life

Some tiring tasks:

DOING THE LAUNDRY. The Greeks send slaves like you to wash their clothes in streams on the edge of town.

SHOP WORK. If your owner runs a business, you'll have to help in the shop, even if it sells smelly cheese or slimy fish.

COOKING LESSONS. To make stew, chop meat, onions, garlic and herbs, add water and boil for hours.

At home, you had horses to carry heavy loads. But here, in the busy city, most of the fetching and carrying is done by slaves. Several times a day your owner's wife sends you into town on errands. She's a respectable citizen's wife, so she stays indoors in the *gunaikeion* (women's quarters). You have to make your way through the crowds along with other shoppers and slaves. You stagger under the weight of pottery jars full of water, huge baskets of shopping or loads of dripping wet laundry. People jostle you and make rude jokes. You feel as if your arms will drop off from sheer exhaustion. Then you're sent out again!

YOU CARRY goods made by your owner's slaves to the market to sell.

YOU BRING BACK fresh food from the market stalls every day.

She was needing a wash!

Ho ho

Tee hee

Handy hint

Don't go shopping in the rain – you get less for your money that way! Dry goods, like grain, soak up the rainwater. They become heavier, so cost more.

splash!

19

Down on the farm

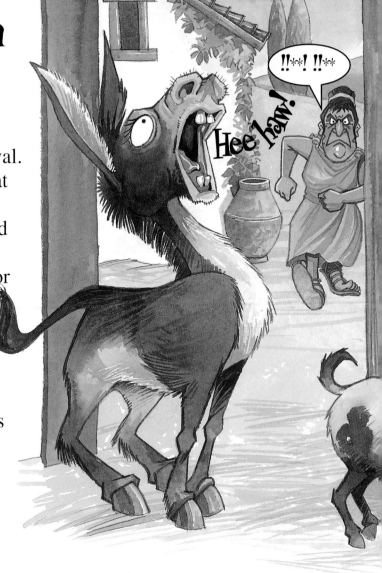

Athens is surrounded by farmland. The food grown, gathered and hunted here is essential for the city's survival. Even the smallest farm has at least one slave and the large farms have dozens. Slaves do all the hard work – preparing the soil, planting and harvesting the crops, and storing them for winter use. They also care for the animals, make olive oil, wine and cheese, and gather wild foods. The Greek countryside is beautiful but harsh. The land is hilly, stony and prone to earthquakes and there are snakes, wolves and bears. It's very hot in summer, but windy and wet in winter.

The farming year

LATE SPRING. You help with haymaking – drying grass for the animals' food.

SUMMER. You winnow the wheat and barley, separating the grain from the chaff.

LATE SUMMER. You use sticks to beat the olive trees so that the fruit falls to the ground.

WHEN THE OLIVES have been crushed to make oil, you pour it into jars.

AUTUMN. You go to the forests to gather berries, nuts and mushrooms.

oooWWWww!

Chomp!

Handy hint

Don't walk in the fields alone. You might be kidnapped by other farmers on the lookout for extra slaves.

Slurp!

WINTER. You look at the cheeses made earlier in the year. Are they maturing, or full of maggots?

EARLY SPRING. You look after the newborn animals. They're always hungry!

JUST IGNORE the rude remarks of the male farm workers and slaves. They're a rough bunch! But their lives are hard, too. They have to work outside in all weathers, ploughing, sowing seeds, harvesting crops and tending sheep and goats on the wild mountain-sides.

21

Lucky you! A good home

The best you can get

You might be lucky and be purchased by a good owner. Some slave owners are kindly by nature. Others find that slaves work better if they are treated well. They give their slaves good food, a comfortable bed and decent clothes.

A KIND OWNER will treat his slaves like friends. (A bad owner will treat them like animals or worse.)

DEATHBED FREEDOM. Your owner might set you free as he lies dying. If he doesn't, you'll be inherited by his son.

THE CHANCE TO SAVE. If your owner has trained you in a skill, he might let you keep some of your earnings to buy your freedom.

Soldier *Doctor* *Teacher*

However, even in the best homes, female slaves like you are not treated equally to men. You cannot do jobs like medicine, teaching or money-changing, or learn crafts such as pottery, building and stone-carving. You will never equal the male slaves who work for the city government as policemen and *dokimastai* (market officials).

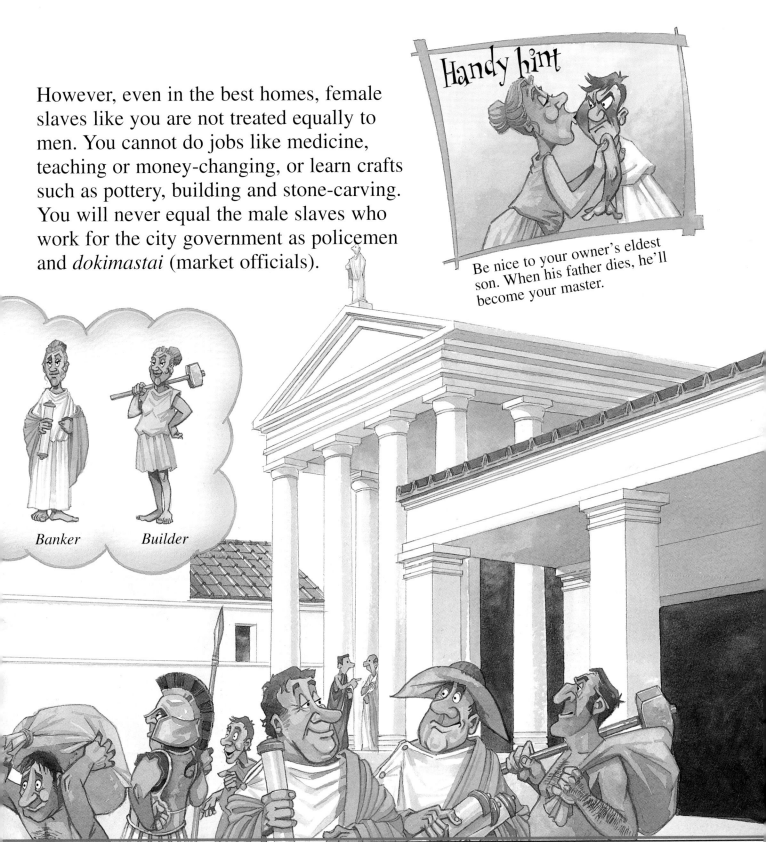

Handy hint

Be nice to your owner's eldest son. When his father dies, he'll become your master.

Banker　　*Builder*

Lowest of the low

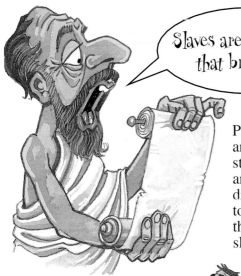

Slaves are possessions that breathe...

PHILOSOPHERS are scholars who study the world around them and discuss the best way to live. This is what they say about slaves (above)!

ALL MALE GREEK CITIZENS have to serve as soldiers. Each man provides his own weapons and armour and a male slave to carry them. Women slaves won't do.

A s a slave, you are one of the lowest-ranking people in Greece. People say that slaves are objects, with no human dignity at all. As a female slave, you are doubly disadvantaged, because the ancient Greeks believe that all women are less important and intelligent than men. They are valued for two things only: their skill at running a household and their ability to produce children. Greek marriages are arranged by families to bring wealth or honour, so the men do not expect to love their wives. For companionship, many husbands turn to female entertainers, called *hetairai*, and female slaves.

Slave rights!

YOU can't vote, serve on juries or debate government plans.

YOU can't take time off, rest if you are ill or leave your workplace.

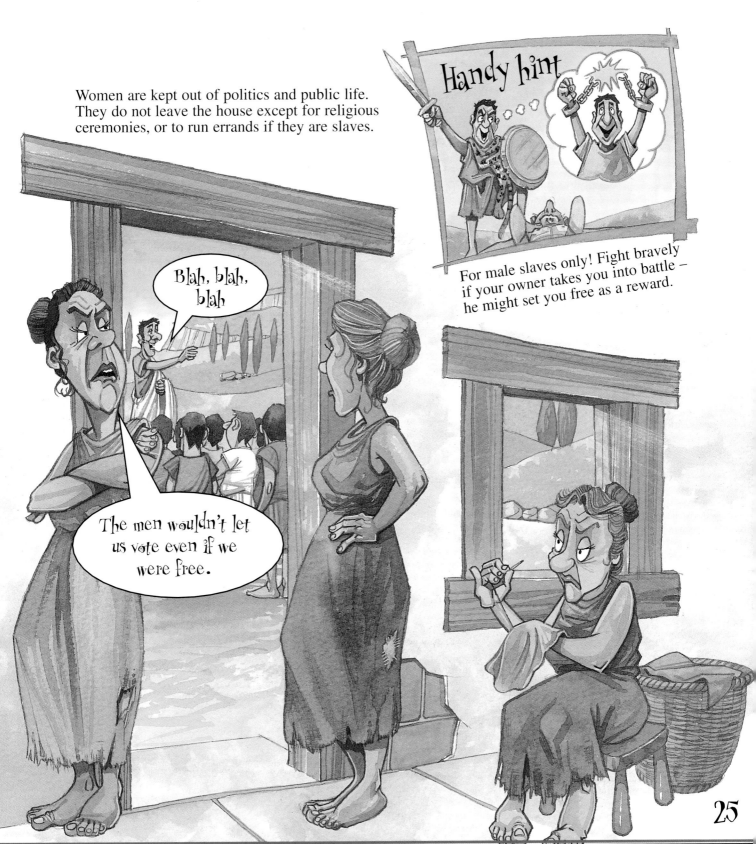

Women are kept out of politics and public life. They do not leave the house except for religious ceremonies, or to run errands if they are slaves.

For male slaves only! Fight bravely if your owner takes you into battle – he might set you free as a reward.

Behave – or you'll be punished!

Heed these warnings:

IF YOU RUN AWAY, you'll be brought back in chains, unless you reach a temple and claim sanctuary from the gods.

Ancient Greek law states that men are masters of their own homes and of everyone living there. They have the right to punish their slaves for laziness, rudeness, theft or telling lies. Disobedience by slaves is an especially serious crime. Like everyone else in the household, it is a slave's duty to be loyal to the man in charge.

YOU'LL BE BADLY BEATEN if your owner gets angry with you. But few slaves are actually beaten to death. They cost too much to replace.

YOUR OWNER will sell you to whoever offers the best price if he no longer trusts you. You'll have no say in the matter.

TO BREAK your disobedient spirit you'll be locked up for days in a dark room, with just bread and water.

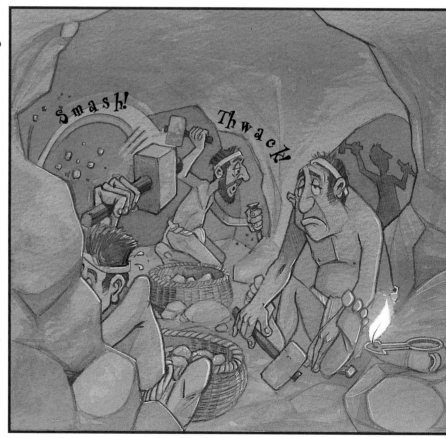

Owners are responsible for any crimes their slaves commit. If you do something wrong, your owner will have to pay a fine. But don't think that this means you will get away without punishment! You will be beaten, locked up or sold. For male slaves, the punishment can be even worse. They could be sent to work in the deep, dark silver mines, where the heat is stifling and the air is full of poisonous fumes.

Keep your clothes on in the mine. They'll make you hot and sweaty, but they'll stop poisonous chemicals seeping into your skin.

Haul away!

SILVER dug by 40,000 slaves in the mines at Laureion has made Athens the richest city in Greece. The Athenians use it for beautiful coins and to pay for a fleet of fast warships.

27

It's all over! Your life ends

You are old and worried about dying. Like your owners, you believe that a funeral is very important as it marks the beginning of your new life after death. It should be performed by your family, with all the proper prayers and ceremonies. Unless you are carefully laid to rest, your spirit will not be able to break free but will haunt the graveside or the house where you died.

IN YOUR SCYTHIAN HOMELAND, you would have been buried with your jewellery, mirror, weapons, and sewing tools for use in the afterlife. Here you will die alone and be buried with nothing. How will your spirit survive? As a slave, you've been unhappy in this life. Now it looks as if you will be wretched for all eternity.

How will you be remembered?

IF SLAVES DROP DEAD from exhaustion, they are buried where they fall. As a female slave, you're lucky. You're more likely to die at your owner's home.

A SIMPLE BURIAL is the best most slaves can hope for. You'll be laid to rest in an unmarked grave, with no funeral ceremonies or prayers.

DON'T EXPECT to be mourned after your death! You'll hardly be cold in your grave before your master buys new slaves to replace you.

IF YOU'RE A FAVOURITE slave, you may be portrayed on your owner's wife's tombstone. Now people will remember you as well as her.

Glossary

Agora The marketplace — a large open space in the center of ancient Greek cities and towns.

Asia Minor The area of land known today as Turkey.

Barbarian Anyone who was not a Greek. The Greeks believed that all barbarians were uncivilized.

Brand To make a mark on someone's skin with a red-hot iron.

Chaff The dry husks surrounding grains of wheat, oats, and barley.

Civet A strong-smelling substance produced by large, wild cats. Used for making perfumes.

Democracy A system of government where the people of a country have power.

Dokimastai Market officials.

Drachma A common Greek coin. In the late 5th century B.C., it was the average wage for a skilled day's work.

Fleeces The wooly coats cut from sheep.

Gunaikeion The private rooms used by women in Greek homes.

Hetairai Educated, elegant unmarried women who were companions and sometimes advisors to wealthy and powerful men.

Nomad A person who lives a wandering lifestyle, moving from place to place.

Oiketai Household slaves.

Philosophers Scholars who study the world around them and discuss the best way to live. Many ancient Greek philosophers' writings are still read today.

Ransom Money paid to set a captive person free.

Sanctuary A safe place recognized by law, often situated in temples and other holy sites.

Scythians People who lived to the north of the Black Sea, in the land known today as southern Russia and Kazakhstan. Rich, noble Scythians were horse riders and probably nomadic; other Scythians lived in farming villages.

Thrace The area of land known today as Bulgaria and Romania.

Winnow To throw ears of wheat, oats, or barley in the air to separate the grains from the chaff.

Xenos A foreigner.

Index

The Games

The Greeks invented athletic contests and held them in honour of their gods. The most famous games were at Olympia, a town in southwest Greece. These took place every four years, and it was in imitation of them that the modern Olympic Games were started in 1896.

The ancient Olympics seem to have begun in the early 700s BC, in honour of the god Zeus. They were open to athletes from all Greek cities, near and far.

Foreigners were not allowed to compete, and women were forbidden from even watching.

As in today's Olympics, some events carried more prestige than others. The most respected of all was the footrace over one length of the stadium – about 192 metres (210 yards). There were also contests in jumping, throwing the javelin and discus, chariot racing, running in armour, wrestling, boxing and a ferocious form of brawling known as the *pankration*.

Olympia

(1) Temple of Zeus; (2) training ground; (3) stadium; (4) hippodrome (for equestrian races); (5) treasuries; (6) Temple of Hera (Zeus's wife)

Did you know?

Pankration, a mixture of boxing and wrestling, had almost no rules. Competitors were allowed to choke and punch each other, even when they were on the floor. Fighters are known to have died from their injuries. However, it was forbidden to kill opponents in the wrestling or boxing matches, either deliberately or accidentally. Gouging the eyes, and biting or breaking the fingers of the opponent, were also forbidden.

Top ancient Greeks

- **Alexander the Great** was called 'the Great' because he conquered more lands than anyone before him and became the overall ruler of Greece.

- **Pythagoras** was a philosopher and mathematician who developed a theory on right-angled triangles.

- **Homer** was the most famous of the Greek epic poets. He wrote the epic poems *The Iliad* and *The Odyssey*.

- **Socrates** was the first of the great Greek philosophers. He is considered by many to be the founder of Western philosophy.

Spartans at war

Greek city-states were rivals and were often at war. There were also defensive wars against foreign enemies, especially Persia. Within city-states, civil unrest broke out between rich and poor, opposing political parties, or masters and slaves.

In the 6th century BC, the Persians were carving out an empire for themselves. They sparked a series of clashes with the Greek city-states that lasted over 50 years. During the Persian Wars, the Spartans and Athenians fought together to defend Greece, but the two city-states could not have been more different, and were often at war with each other. Athens was a centre of culture and learning, whereas Sparta was a military state where the majority of people were slaves and all the male citizens were soldiers.

Spartan children were treated harshly and disciplined strongly. Their childhood was meant to prepare them for the rigours of later life and military service. They were taught to jeer at the weak and learned how to be sly. They were taught to steal, even taking holy food from temples.

Becoming a man

At the age of 18, Greek men became *ephebes*. This meant they were ready to become citizens, but first they had to prove themselves worthy. Ephebes had to live by strict rules for two years, including a period of required military service. Learning to be a soldier was tough.